Parenting Gifted Children to Support Optimal Development

Stephen T. Schroth and Jason A. Helfer

Cheryll M. Adams, Series Editor

T0056254

National Association for Gifted Children
1331 H Street, NW, Suite 1001
Washington, DC 20005
202-785-4268
http://www.nagc.org

TABLE OF CONTENTS

INTRODUCTION

For many parents, guardians, or other caretakers of gifted children, scenarios such as these are familiar:

Bridget is 4 and has been reading for a year and a half. Although her older sisters did well in school, Bridget has demonstrated an even quicker mastery of all that is put in front of her—she began talking at 5 months, knew her colors and shapes by the time of her first birthday, and has shown a keen interest in a variety of subjects, such as the solar system and the music of Bach. Although both of Bridget's parents graduated from top-tier law schools, they are concerned that they are not doing enough to support their child's learning and development. A neighbor mentioned her belief that children should have begun music and foreign language instruction by the age of 4, which caused Bridget's parents to worry because they have not provided instruction in those areas for their daughter.

Alejandro is 8 years old. He did not speak English until he entered Kindergarten but has read all of the Harry Potter books and is mastering algebra through an afterschool tutoring program led by some local college students. Although his father speaks English, Alejandro's mother and grandmother do not, and Spanish is spoken exclusively in the home. Alejandro's father works in a box factory, and his mother is a homemaker. His parents do not have a great deal of formal schooling, but are highly respectful of education and very deferential to teachers, a group whom they hold in high regard. While they try to support Alejandro academically, his parents worry if they are doing all they can for him.

Christopher, 11 years old, is a middle child with two sisters. He and his sisters live with their unmarried mother in a small town in the rural Midwest. Christopher excels as an athlete, playing competitive football, basketball, and baseball. Christopher gets excellent marks in school and enjoys playing the guitar with his uncle. Christopher's school offers no special education or gifted education services. Although his mother is a high school dropout, she had a good paying job until recently, when the appliance manufacturer for whom she worked closed its factory in their town. Now working the night shift at a gas station, she worries that she does not have the time or talents needed to support Christopher's needs.

Kahlil is 14 years of age and lives with his mother and grandmother. Working two jobs to support Kahlil, his mother is frequently out of the house, leaving his grandmother primarily responsible for his care. Since he was 6, Kahlil has been a member of the choir at his church, and has taken honors track classes since he enrolled in middle school. Kahlil's school houses both a neighborhood-serving academy and a science and technology magnet program that is open to children from around the city. Unlike most of his peers from the neighborhood who attend the academy, Kahlil is enrolled at the science and technology magnet. Recently, Kahlil has complained to his grandmother and mother that he is often the only African American student in his classes, and that he resents having to "act White." Although Kahlil's grandmother and mother want him to get the background necessary for him to do well in college, they also seek to provide him with a learning environment in which he is comfortable with his peers. They are unsure how best to proceed.

Je'Ana is 17 years old and beginning her senior year at a large suburban high school. Although she is in the top quarter of her class, her scores on achievement tests indicate that she is performing well below her potential. While she has a great deal of ability in mathematics and the sciences, Je'Ana prefers to take classes in English, social studies, and the arts. During her junior year, she became very involved in the school newspaper, and attended a summer camp for budding journalists over the summer break. Je'Ana's biracial parents are both college educated and want her to more fully realize her potential. They also are hopeful that Je'Ana's college search will permit her to find a school where she is able to develop her passions while also finding employment after graduation.

Successfully dealing with the challenges related to child rearing is a frequent challenge for many parents.[1] Although the children described in the previous scenarios face different challenges, their parents all struggle to find answers that will work for their children and their families.

The care and tending of gifted children, while rewarding, often takes parents by surprise, especially if they have not had previous experience with the highly able. Many parents consult books and other resources for answers on how best to parent their gifted children. Despite these efforts, parents of gifted children have limited access to resources that focus upon their gifted child's cognitive, physical, and social and emotional development. Parents from historically underrepresented groups find even fewer resources dedicated to the parent role in the learning and development of their children. Discussions with friends seldom provide responses that focus on the specific academic or social and emotional needs of gifted children, and many teachers have scant training in how to advise parents on their role in the learning and development of gifted children. As a result, many parents of gifted children have unanswered questions about how best to work with and support their children. These questions include: Am I pushing my child too hard? If I don't provide enrichment for my child, will she fall behind? What are the best activities in which I can enroll my son? How can I ask my child's teacher about ways she can provide him with more challenging activities? When is the best time to look for afterschool or summer programs for my child? Why do I need to worry about my child's social and emotional needs? Who can help me obtain answers to these questions?

Giftedness, of course, is a changing concept and one that historically was seen as a biologically grounded label for those with high levels of intelligence who were able to easily participate in advanced and accelerated coursework. This conception of giftedness has expanded greatly in recent years. Many now view children who exhibit advanced skills in problem solving, creative and critical thinking, leadership, academic aptitude, performance in the arts, invention, or a variety of other areas as gifted. Giftedness is often seen as the interaction of various aspects of the brain such as cognition, emotion, intuition, and physical sensing rather than just analytical abilities. These interactions result in a variety of characteristics of gifted children that differentiate them from their age peers. These characteristics result in unique needs, which must be met for a child to fully develop his or her potential. While giftedness is a broad concept, this NAGC Select will focus on children with advanced cognitive abilities or the potential for exhibiting advanced cognitive abilities.

A gifted child's talent is created by the continuous interaction between his or her genetic dispositions and the

4

environment in which he or she lives. Although genes play an important role in determining the possibilities for children's lives, the environment in which children live changes them neurologically and biologically. This makes opportunities for appropriate challenge crucial to ensure that talents and abilities are developed rather than lost. Thus, high levels of actualized ability result from *both* inherited abilities and the opportunities to develop them. Furthermore, recent research has highlighted the importance of beliefs in the malleability of ability through effort as contributing to full development of potential. Providing gifted children with proper support and appropriate levels of challenge will assist in their development.[2]

Parents affect their children's long-term development through their attitudes, behaviors, and expectations. Notions regarding success and failure, aspirations and expectations for achievement, responsibility and self-control, the importance of effort, and family environment all shape a gifted child's opportunities for a high level of development. Parents can provide an environment for gifted children that offers access to new ideas and information, enthusiasm for learning, ways to attack problems, the development of persistence, and an understanding that certain actions have probable consequences and results. By providing opportunities for learning, reducing tension for the gifted child, and acknowledging the child's accomplishments— particularly through recognition of ability *and* effort— parents can increase the likelihood for optimal development. Ideally, a great deal of support for these efforts would come from the student's school. However, many schools do not offer specific programming for their most able students, and teachers in the regular education classroom often lack appropriate training in how to nurture such talents. This situation leaves many parents of gifted children feeling isolated and uncertain about how best to proceed.

Fortunately, there are resources and materials readily available to assist parents in supporting gifted learners at school and at home. We will examine how the parents of Bridget, Alejandro, Christopher, Kahlil, and Je'Ana can learn more about the characteristics of their gifted children and how to provide opportunity and support in their development and learning. We will also provide information on programming options that are available both within and outside of school and suggestions for maximizing the social and emotional development of highly talented children. Suggestions also will be made for families whose school districts that have comprehensive gifted education programs and services and those that do not. It is also important to remember that gifted learners are still children, and while they may exhibit special cognitive abilities or other talents, many of their psychomotor and affective characteristics will mirror those of their age peers. Combining a variety of approaches and strategies together to assist the whole child's development often works best.

CHARACTERISTICS AND DEVELOPMENT

Gifted children often demonstrate characteristics that distinguish them from their peers, and consequently, require different learning interventions and supports to maximize their potential.[3] The public's knowledge of these characteristics and appropriate responses, regrettably, is often formed by outdated stereotypes based almost solely on achievement. These beliefs tend to color many teachers' actions, which are predicated upon the (mistaken) understanding that gifted children are self-sufficient learners who need little support. Although many school districts do not support the formal identification of children as gifted before the third grade, many children in pre-school or Kindergarten settings are gifted and demonstrating behaviors that are wholly different than most of the other children in their classrooms. And many children display gifted characteristics before entering any formal school setting.

Although those characteristics vary by child, some tendencies are seen frequently across the population of gifted and talented learners. How the characteristics of gifted children are described depends to some degree on how *giftedness* is defined. A variety of conceptions of giftedness exist, with many similarities but some significant differences as well.[4] The way in which giftedness is conceptualized greatly affects those children identified as gifted, as well as the program options deemed appropriate and necessary. Gifted learners frequently demonstrate rapid learning rates and the ability to understand complex and abstract concepts, surpassing their age peers in basic skills. As a result, gifted children should be exposed to new and

7

challenging information, as well as have access to more advanced curriculum and to peers who operate at the same speed and depth of learning. Gifted children's well-developed memories, intense interest in certain subjects, and use of creative and critical thinking, processing, and problem-solving skills often provide justification for special programming or other enrichment settings where these characteristics can be fully nurtured. Gifted children benefit from the chance to pursue inquiries and to set and evaluate their own priorities when solving problems at a more advanced level. Especially important for gifted children are exposure to alternative methods of solving problems and solutions to those problems, abstractions, the consequences of choices, and the opportunities to draw generalizations and to test them.

Gifted children often demonstrate the use of advanced thinking, processing, and problem-solving skills at an early age. From an early age, gifted children often demonstrate a high degree of motivation when tackling new or familiar tasks, and reveal insight and flexibility in their thought processes. Consequently, instruction in creative thinking and problem-solving strategies benefit gifted children, but these are also skills and processes to which all children should be exposed.[5] The key for gifted students is advanced exposure to these ideas at an individual rate, permission to solve problems in diverse ways, and freedom to pursue individual ideas as far as interest permits. Providing such opportunities are all ways parents can help their children further develop those skills.

Diverse Learners' Characteristics and Needs
When gifted learners come from diverse backgrounds, their characteristics may be subtly different from those

8

assumed in more traditional conceptions of giftedness. Diverse learners, who include children of color, English language learners, students from low-socioeconomic status (SES) backgrounds, and twice-exceptional learners, share many of the characteristics of other gifted children. They may, however, also exhibit some key differences based upon their backgrounds and experiences[6] that parents may need to address in order for the gifted child to receive gifted education services. For example, some diverse gifted learners may need additional content background knowledge, skill training, and support to make up for lack of exposure to advanced opportunities or handicapping conditions that make access to knowledge more difficult. Diverse learners may have communication skills that are different than those to which many teachers are accustomed, which can affect student and parent understanding of the conceptual, procedural, and tacit demands of a rigid curriculum.[7] The students and their parents, for example, may be unaware of how to initiate the research process or the expectation that assignments that are weighted more heavily in grading receive a greater time investment. In some cases, parents may need to emphasize their child's preference for collaborative rather than competitive learning experiences due to a reluctance to stand out from the group and that their traditions, heritage, and beliefs often result in different forms of expression. Also, because many gifted education programs rely on discussion and independent learning rather than specific instructions for required tasks, parents of diverse gifted children may need to be prepared to help their children adjust to a new style of teaching and learning.

Remembering Their Chronological Age

Gifted children, no matter how exceptional, are still children. As such they need to experience literature, activities, and other enrichment that is age appropriate for them. All too often grade school children will read Shakespeare, yet be denied exposure to *Alice in Wonderland, Kidnapped*, and other classic and modern literature that is much more age-relevant While very young children can demonstrate skills and talents that indicate they are gifted, attempts to hurry gifted children through the process of growing up can deny them some of the many pleasures of being a child, as well as cause them to miss some of the key experiences necessary to mature and develop.[8] Introducing activities that are centered on age-appropriate materials, but that allow gifted children to engage in critical and creative thinking, is often a better approach.

Theorists such as Bloom and Montessori have written of sensitive periods that are crucial in an individual's development.[9] *Sensitive periods* are those stages of time in which a child concentrates mainly on one aspect of his or her environment or learning and excludes everything else. Montessori identified the following sensitive periods that all children experience from birth to age 6:

- Sensitive period for movement (birth to 4 years);
- Sensitive period for refinement of the senses (birth to 5 years);
- Sensitive period for language (birth to 6 years);
- Sensitive period for weaning (5 to 6 months);
- Sensitive period for order (18 months to 2 years);

- Sensitive period for manners and courtesies (2 to 6 years); and

- Sensitive period for numbers (4 to 5.5 years).

These sensitive periods can be viewed as basic guidelines as to when a child is ready to learn in certain areas and when might be a good time to introduce certain types of concepts to children.

Bloom posited that the environment will most greatly affect the development of certain traits during their sensitive periods and that progressing through some or all of these periods early might indicate giftedness. Others have identified other sensitive periods, including visual complexity (birth to 2 months), hearing (prenatal period to 6 months), and language (18 months to 4 years). Children who exhibit more extensive vocabularies and use complex sentence structure while speaking often demonstrate higher levels of mental ability, although early language development is not always present in gifted students and adults. Some have theorized that early reading represents an extension of early language development and also indicates advanced development. Certainly children who learn to read at an earlier age have the advantage of increased vocabulary and knowledge as a result of their reading.

As gifted children move into school settings, they may experience their first problems of "fit" in an educational context.[10] Many of the skills and much of the knowledge base typical of preschool curriculum have already been mastered by gifted children. As gifted children progress into Kindergarten and the primary grades, they may experience intense boredom unless the curriculum and classroom routines are structured in a way that accommodates their learning differences. Certainly all young children need a curriculum that is abundant in variety and stimulating in process. For gifted children, however, this variety and stimulation are even more essential. In addition, gifted children are likely to benefit from a level of freedom in decisions about their learning that permits more self-direction, experience with abstract concepts, and exposure to the tools and skills necessary to develop skills as writers, mathematicians, historians, scientists, researchers, artists, musicians, and readers. By engaging in more authentic, real-life tasks, young gifted learners are able to participate in work similar to that of practitioners in the various disciplines. Parents should develop strategies to keep the school informed of their children's perceptions of school experiences and be vigilant in providing positive feedback to teacher choices of curriculum or teaching strategies that engage their children in positive learning.

As they reach adolescence many gifted children, much like their age peers, will experience certain worries and anxieties regarding their popularity and how well they "fit in" with their classmates. Parents can help alleviate their gifted children's worries and anxieties with honest discussion in a warm and supportive household. Indeed, gifted children with strong and supportive family relationships experience fewer social concerns than their age peers. Parents might also discuss with their children their above-average intelligence, but also the positive effects of effort that will provide them with effective tools to grapple with struggles and challenges. Parents should also encourage their children to engage in one or more of the other effective tools in grappling with struggles and challenges such as discussing problems with others, learning to identify the way others' actions make them feel, understanding that different people have different strengths, and reading books where characters experience difficulties fitting in with their peers. Parents should also realize that their higher levels of maturity and experience yield much greater foresight than their gifted child has, even if the child is much more intelligent than the parent. Helping to guide one's children is one of the most rewarding parts of life, and parents should never shy away from offering advice and guidance, no matter how intelligent their child.

Responding to the Characteristics of Gifted Students

Bridget's quick rate of learning and easy mastery of complex material indicate skills and talents that demand services from schools and support from her family. Since she is an excellent candidate for early admission to Kindergarten, Bridget's parents might push for the local school district to focus more on her skills than on her chronological age. Many discussions regarding "giftedness" devolve into debates regarding identification, but Bridget will be best served if all involved concentrate upon providing her the services that best meet her needs. Bridget's parents will also support their daughter's gifts by investigating exhibits and enrichment programs available at local museums, symphony orchestras, and other cultural institutions.

Alejandro's parents need to advocate for him at his school, helping his teachers and others to view his bilingualism as a tremendous strength. If possible, it would be beneficial for Alejandro to receive instruction in the nuances of written Spanish, as many children who are native speakers struggle with this portion of the language later in life. As his mother sometimes writes poetry and other short pieces in Spanish, she has begun working with him so that he can build and maintain his writing skills in that language.

Alejandro's interests in reading and algebra should be encouraged by involvement at the local public library and participation in other afterschool, weekend, and summer programs for gifted and talented students.

Christopher is thriving and engaged in activities that support his athletic and musical talents. His mother might contemplate how best to get Christopher involved in pursuits that also nurture his cognitive abilities. While this is more difficult to do in a rural setting than some other areas, Christopher's mother would do well to determine what activities are available and to get him involved in one or two that are of interest. In addition to those sponsored by schools, many smaller communities have historical sites, museums, symphony orchestras, or arts cooperatives that offer educational programming and that welcome volunteers. After some exploration into available options, Christopher began volunteering at a railroad museum, where he assists in setting up exhibits and writing promotional materials for the organization.

Kahlil's grandmother and mother should find a support group, either through his school or a local or statewide gifted organization, which can provide them with insights and validation regarding their parenting choices. Their decision to push Kahlil to pursue the best educational avenues available is providing him with options he might otherwise be denied. Kahlil's grandmother and mother should, however, seek additional ways for him to interact with other children and adult mentors who are also African American, perhaps through their church or other neighborhood organizations. If available, Kahlil's grandmother and mother should also seek out cultural heritage centers or museums devoted to African American achievement in all fields where he can learn about and identify with others like him.

Je'Ana's strong preference for the arts and language should not worry her parents, as gifted children often demonstrate a passion for one area of learning over all others. While her parents wished to expose Je'Ana to a variety of fields when she was younger to determine where her interests lay, once this was established it is fine for her to concentrate upon those areas where she is highly talented. As she begins her college search process, Je'Ana and her parents should look for schools where she will be able to engage in the arts and literature, and where her passions will be supported and nurtured. This might include schools that include a studio term or other experience where students can engage in sustained interaction with their field of study.

Suggestions

When considering the characteristics and developments of gifted children, parents would be well-served to keep the following in mind:

- High levels of ability are the result of the interaction between genetics and the environment, making a child's preschool years an essential time for learning.

- High levels of cognitive development cannot occur without a high level of interaction between the child's inherited potentialities and appropriately enriching experiences. To ensure that this occurs, parents and families should provide access to conversations that encourage observations of the environment, parks, zoos, museums, and other activities that will provide material with which he or she can interact. These need not be expensive or costly opportunities. They can occur in free and open spaces such as a walk in the woods or a park where the child can be asked to point out how plants are similar or dissimilar.

- Knowledge about the characteristics and needs of gifted learners will help parents better understand and support their gifted children and address potential problems that may arise. Parents and families can learn about these characteristics and needs through websites such as that of the National Association for Gifted Children or other groups that support gifted students, by browsing the local school website or Hoagie's Gifted Education Page, through a range of publications, or by joining a local parent advocacy group so that they can better support their child at home and at school.

- Families who intend to enroll their gifted child in preschool should look for a preschool curriculum that features rich variety and provides stimulating processes for *all* children. Look for evidence that the instructional pace can accommodate the rapid learning of gifted children.

- Parents should be aware of the sensitive and critical periods of development so they can ensure their gifted child is in an environment that helps develop sensory, mental, and motor skills as fully and rapidly as possible.

- A child's gifts and talents are more likely to be actualized with the encouragement, environmental opportunities, and support provided by families, teachers, and other important adults. While a child may not have immediate and constant support from all at the same time, a child with consistent encouragement and stimulus— regardless of source — will likely benefit greatly.

FAMILY DYNAMICS

Parents of the gifted often work with their children in a variety of settings, including the home, school, enrichment programs, and other environments. None of these settings is more important for the positive development of a gifted child's cognitive, affective, and physical skills than the home.[11] At home, gifted children interact with their parents, siblings, and other family and non-family members in ways that affect their growth and development. It is important for parents to be aware of the ways in which others, including siblings, interact with a gifted child as the interaction can cause joy, or stress, for all members of the household. Gifted children always need the support and encouragement of the adults in their lives, although how that support and encouragement manifests will vary depending upon the age and needs of the gifted child. Family dynamics will be improved if all members of the family modify their behaviors in ways that will support the growth and development of all the children.

Almost all parenting styles can be described as falling within one of four categories: uninvolved, permissive, authoritative, and authoritarian. *Uninvolved parenting* can be characterized by parents who make few demands on their children, exhibit low responsiveness to their needs, and offer little communication. Although their child's basic needs are fulfilled, these parents are generally detached from their child's life. *Permissive parenting* can be considered to include parents who rarely discipline their children and who possess relatively low expectations regarding their maturity and self-control. Permissive parents are more responsive than they are demanding, tend to be non-traditional and lenient in their approach, encourage their children to self-regulate, and are non-confrontational. *Authoritative parenting* demands that rules and guidelines be followed, yet is also responsive to children and includes a willingness to take questions. When their children fail to follow the rules, authoritative parents tend to nurture them so they will make the correct decision the next time and forgive misconduct rather than punish misbehavior. This type of parenting, which is assertive but not intrusive or restrictive, is the best for allowing children to feel supported and to foster communication. *Authoritarian parenting* encompasses practices that place high demands upon children with low levels of responsiveness. Authoritarian parents establish strict rules, which if broken results in harsh punishment for their children. Little time is spent explaining to children why certain rules have been implemented, and if their children question these, discussion is quickly curtailed. Authoritarian parents are interested in obedience from their children and the status derived from their accomplishments.

The choice, conscious or subconscious, of a particular parenting style has great consequences for family dynamics, especially with regard to a child's happiness, social competence, and self-esteem. Those homes with uninvolved parenting styles rank the lowest across all domains, with children often lacking self-control, having low self-esteem, and being less competent than their peers with regard to interactions. Those with permissive parenting styles result in children who rank low in happiness and self-regulation, being more likely to experience problems with authority and tending to perform poorly in school. In households that emphasize authoritarian parenting styles children may be obedient and proficient, but these children also rank lower in happiness, social competence, and self-esteem than do other children who were reared in authoritative homes.

Homes with authoritative parenting styles most often provide gifted children with the level of support necessary for making good decisions on their own, developing strong interpersonal skills, and having a sense of accomplishment from being able to do certain things successfully.

Family Composition

In families with more than one child, it is important to remember that each child is unique and will benefit from parental support that reflect those differences.[12] Much as teachers differentiate instruction in the classroom, parents must sometimes differentiate their parenting so that the needs of all their children are addressed. Parents must be careful to observe and attend to those signals that indicate differences between their children. These differences may involve the type and amount of supervision, support, discipline, or nurturing that a child needs, and extends into varied interests and personalities. Parents should concentrate on providing a home environment that makes each child feel safe to become who he or she is destined to be. One child's needs should not be viewed as more important or significant than another's, and the accomplishments of all should be celebrated, regardless of whether they occur in the classroom, in performance halls, or on the playing field. The opportunities extended to each child should stem from his or her characteristics, interests, talents, skills, needs, and strengths. As children become older, they should become "junior partners" in the selection of those opportunities.

In single-parent households, it can be challenging to ensure that the gifted child receives the same level of support, care, enrichment, and attention and the same opportunities without the assistance of other caring, supportive adults. As with dual-parent families, the single parent might join a group comprised of the parents of gifted children so that ideas can be shared and support provided with regard to issues related to child rearing.[13] If friends or family members have parented a gifted child, they might also be a useful resource for discussions regarding decisions and choices.

Continuum of Parenting Support

Gifted children, from early childhood through high school, benefit from a continuum of parenting support and nurturing that changes as appropriate to the child's skills and developmental differences at various points in time.[14] At a very early age, gifted children spend most of their time at home or in facilities that provide childcare. The young gifted child's parents are the individuals most likely to notice those behaviors that are characteristic of highly talented children. The parents of young gifted children also are often also providing enrichment, either in the home or through outings to parks, libraries, museums, or other places that will expand the young learner's horizons. It is not always necessary that outings or in-home enrichment experiences be academic in nature: the emphasis should be on *how* to use certain tools, process information, and discuss what has been observed rather than upon the quantity of tools or the recall of information. Visual images, especially those that lead to storytelling or other creative activities, are useful tools for in-home enrichment. For example, having young gifted children draw a picture or create a song that retells certain aspects of a picture book read to them illustrate extension activities. Through all activities, parents should ask their children what they are seeing, feeling, and hearing. These types of questions will help gifted children make sense of the world around them and to learn which avenues they wish to pursue further.

As children grow older, more enrichment occurs outside of the parent's purview. Despite this change, the parents of gifted children are wise to continue to ask questions about perceptions of and from these experiences. Parents should also monitor those experiences that excite and interest their child more than others. Not all children need or want to pursue all things, as being "well rounded" is not a requirement for being gifted. Indeed, intense interest in certain subjects should be encouraged, so the child who enjoys astronomy will benefit from visits to planetariums, books about the solar system, and videos about space exploration while her brother who is passionate about opera may not. As students enter middle school and high school, this winnowing of interests will often accelerate. In many school districts, services for gifted children cease at or about the sixth grade, as it is assumed that the honors classes offered in middle school will provide sufficient stimulation. This change makes it even more important that parents carefully monitor their children's classes and provide enrichment opportunities through other avenues when appropriate.

Gifted high school students often have acquired a level of mastery of certain skills that make engagement in out-of-school opportunities to work with others with similar levels of skill an appropriate option. This might include music camps, science weekends, or other such activities, many of which offer scholarship support or reduced fees. While many gifted children may have begun participating in such offerings in elementary or middle school, once they reach the high school level these explorations increase in intensity, frequency, and duration. For example, where many music programs for elementary and middle grade children concentrate on providing opportunities to explore the discipline, those for high school students focus instead on honing those skills that will be needed by musicians for success at the professional level. These experiences are important for gifted children as they are often highly driven, non-conforming, divergent thinkers making them unlike many of their age peers. Additionally, because many gifted children can excel in two or more fields, they often have multiple potential paths for future careers. Gifted high school students who exhibit such multipotentialities should have the opportunity to explore a variety of disciplines so that they may better determine where their interests lie.

Gifted high school students might also benefit from pursuing internships in academic or vocational settings. Internships permit students the opportunity to explore a variety of industries, professions, and settings, allowing them a chance to determine if they see a place for themselves in the field while simultaneously acquiring skills. Internships for high school students may last a period as short as a month, or may extend throughout the school year. Teachers and parents must take great care to ensure that the gifted child is engaged in constructive work during the internship. In some areas, schools have moved from encouraging internships to requiring service learning hours. Again, while these opportunities can be very beneficial, it is important for parents to understand the specific skills and other benefits to the gifted child in a service learning placement. Also, although often ignored, paid employment opportunities are often a tremendous way for gifted adolescents to develop a strong work ethic, a sense of time management, and an understanding of the hierarchical structure of most work places. Jobs also allow gifted high school students to acquire the funds to pay for other interests.

In their schools, adolescent gifted students should take advantage of whatever honors curriculum is offered by their school district. Many times high schools offer Advanced Placement (AP) or International Baccalaureate (IB) classes, which offer increased rigor and the opportunity to achieve college credit. Some high schools also offer dual enrollment programs, where students are permitted to take courses at a local college or university in lieu of a high school course for the same subject. High school students should also begin to think about college applications and possible careers. It is *not* necessary to apply to a host of different colleges and universities, and a list of five or six suitable options will be more easily compiled if this process begins early, say at the beginning of junior year. For gifted students interested in pursuing certain majors in college, more careful and earlier preparation might be necessary. Those interested in pursuing studies in foreign languages, music, dance, theatre, visual arts, creative writing, mathematics, or the sciences may be well served by ensuring that their high school coursework will support their future endeavors. Many students wishing to enroll in conservatories, for example, must audition for a place in the school, while budding artists must submit a portfolio of their work. Enrolling in a challenging set of classes for all four years of high school will assist gifted children in the admissions process to selective institutions. While some colleges have particular requirements regarding high school coursework, it is important to remember that many excellent schools do not. Cal Tech, for example, asks only for four years of math, three of English, chemistry, and physics. Gifted students interested in particular programs, colleges, or universities should investigate the entrance requirements as early as possible to avoid unpleasant surprises later in the process.

Balancing the Family's and the Child's Needs

Parenting is more of an art than a science. While the balance will change from time to time, parents of gifted children should consider the unique characteristics of their gifted child, their family as a whole, and their own personal desires.[15] Parents often make decisions at the spur of the moment, and should appreciate they will sometimes make mistakes. Being forthright and honest with children helps them to understand that while their well-being is of paramount concern, there are times when they might not get what they want. No particular template exists for parenting gifted children, so parents need to be willing to experiment and search for ways to stimulate and challenge their children. It is always important to remember that gifted children are not adults, and they lack the wisdom and experience of older persons. Gifted children need parents to set limits and to provide them with mentoring and modeling the behaviors expected from the family unit. Rearing gifted children can be immensely rewarding, especially when the focus remains on the relationship between parent and child.

Parenting in the 21st century, unfortunately, often involves a great expenditure of time, money, and other resources to match the child with opportunities. For parents with more than one child, such expenditures can be exhausting or cost prohibitive or both. It is important that parents facing such a dilemma remember that more is not always more, and that opportunities need to be balanced with a program of action that is reasonable both in terms of cost and time commitment. Many wonderful opportunities are available at no or low cost, and it is certainly reasonable to consider the amount of driving time or other factors when deciding between multiple options. A program that offers services for middle school and elementary school children might be a better option for the family with 9 and 12-year-old children than two separate programs located some distance apart. Unless compelling reasons exist why a child must be enrolled in a particular activity or program, considering matters such as time and money makes good sense.

A strong family environment contributes to the social competence of the gifted child. Families that are able to achieve both a sense of cohesiveness, where all make decisions that benefit the common and individual good, and effective communication between family members increases the likelihood that all are satisfied and content. Family environments that are affectionate, respectful, and supportive help gifted children to develop better interpersonal skills and competencies. These positive family environments also permit better peer relationships, in part because the gifted child has acquired constructive and effective ways of interacting with others.

Navigating Family Dynamics

Bridget is the youngest of four girls, with older sisters who are 13, 11, and 6. All of her sisters are bright and do well in school, although none is as academically precocious as Bridget. Rachel, the oldest sister, loves to play the viola and is a member of a string quartet. The next oldest, Katie, is an all-around athlete who loves soccer and basketball, while Mary, the second youngest, prefers engaging in the visual arts. When planning for activities for their children, Bridget's parents make a schedule that ensures that each girl gets approximately 25% of the time spent devoted to one child. As a result, Rachel has an audience at her concerts, Katie has fans cheering her on at her games, and Mary has participants at her art shows. With these patterns established, Bridget can have someone take her to story time at the library without resentment. Similarly, the parents attempt to equalize the time spent chauffeuring children to lessons and events. While each child participates in different types of activities and receives support targeted to her needs, all get attention and love from their mother and father.

Alejandro has a one-year-old sister, Marisol, whom he loves dearly. Although Marisol is not yet able to talk much and has just started walking, Alejandro loves to play with her and takes great pride in being a big brother. Alejandro loves to read to Marisol. Alejandro's parents should encourage this behavior and suggest that he extend the activity by telling Marisol stories that he creates, perhaps using props or a felt board to show her his extensions. His parents should also ensure that Alejandro gets some time with them that is just for him, which might include outings to parks or libraries. Alejandro also has some older cousins with whom he likes to play soccer and who provide a peer group for him even though they are several years older and in middle school. This interaction should be encouraged, as many gifted children prefer the company of older children. Achieving a balance between time spent on the gifted child and time spent as a family has many benefits for the child, such as the ripening of stronger relationships among family members, the development of patience, and appreciating the connections between the cognitive and affective aspects of his or her life.

Christopher's mother elected to work the night shift rather than the swing shift at the local gas station convenience mart so that she would be home, and awake, during the time that her children are home from school. Because of this, she has the opportunity to work with Christopher and his sisters to help them complete homework, attend athletic events, and from time to time meet with teachers during the day. Christopher and his sisters Libby (13) and Maddie (9) get along very well together and help each other to finish school projects and take care of chores around the house. While Christopher's mother has made it a priority to find activities for her son that support his cognitive growth, it is equally important that she devote time to finding appropriate endeavors for her daughters to pursue as well. As her work schedule is fairly rigid, it would be helpful to establish a family-school communication routine, which can be especially useful if there are issues that need resolving. Planning for such a scenario will permit the family to devote its energies to resolving conflict, should it arise, by using pre-established procedures.

Kahlil's grandmother worries that her lack of a college education might hinder the support she can give her grandson, as she sometimes feels unqualified to assist him with schoolwork or to answer questions about his education after high school. One of seven children herself, Kahlil's grandmother is the matriarch of an extended family, with many nieces and nephews who have attained a college education. His mother is pursuing classes at a local community college. Although it is important for Kahlil to interact with the rest of his family, his grandmother has a degree of credibility that no one else does. Kahlil loves his grandmother dearly and greatly respects her. When his grandmother accompanies Kahlil to museums or other destinations he is always extra excited because she is along. While other relatives or mentors may be helpful in filling out college applications or providing other advice, there is no substitution for his grandmother's participation in Kahlil's life.

Je'Ana is a strong student, but it took her a while to "find herself" in high school. Although she participated in many different activities when younger, Je'Ana's parents recently have encouraged her to focus on theatre productions at her high school, her school newspaper, and several other artistic pursuits about which she is passionate rather than continuing to devote time to activities (e.g., science camp, swim team) that seem to be of little interest. As gifted children mature, parents may find that it is often better for their gifted child to pursue areas of passion than to dabble in areas that are not of interest.

Suggestions

- The home environment plays a significant role at every stage of a gifted child's development, influencing a child's progress and success. Parents should assess their home environment periodically, determining whether all children in the house are being nurtured and supported as well as possible.

- Using an authoritative parenting style (where independence is balanced with limits, consequences, and expectations) increases the chances that a child will be successful in school and in life and is more successful than using the authoritarian parenting style (where strict rules and expectations provide children few choices or options) or the permissive parenting style (with few rules or expectations).

- Ensuring that the educational program sets contact points for meetings and conferences with parents increases the opportunities for the school to maximize the gifted child's development. Parents should familiarize themselves with their child's school schedule for parent/teacher meetings and request additional in-person or phone contact if they feel these are necessary.

- Schedule time during the week for each child, and ensure that the accomplishments and concerns of each are given equal consideration and attention. Sometimes the simple use of a calendar with times for targeted support for each child written in can assist this effort.

- The gifted child's needs for acceptance, belonging, and a sense of self-esteem are best met by the child's family. Many families schedule a weekly "forum" during which they can discuss accomplishments and concerns that have occurred during the week, thereby increasing communications and opportunities for parents to offer encouragement and support.

PROGRAMMING OPTIONS

Parents are often faced with a variety of choices regarding their child's educational options[16]. While these choices are determined in part by what a particular school or school district has made available, sometimes parents might consider their child's social and emotional needs in determining the best choice for him or her. Although some question the value of providing gifted services, studies have consistently demonstrated that gifted students who receive *any* level of services achieve at higher levels than their gifted peers who receive none. These services can come in a variety of formats, and run the gamut from very expensive to low- or no-cost. Some service models are part-time, while others provide a full-day experience for the gifted child. Parents who know what each service delivery model offers and its attending limitations can better assist their children in finding the appropriate learning setting.

Approaches Common in Schools

Public schools are charged with educating all students in their community with a wide range of special needs that vie for attention. Education of the gifted is one of many competing demands. As many states do not mandate that services be provided to gifted children, and others do not specify what districts are required to provide, many school districts and schools opt not to provide specialized services for gifted children or provide limited services and programs in one contact area for children in only a few grades. As a result many gifted children receive services in the regular classroom from a teacher who differentiates instruction with the intent that each will receive instruction at an appropriate level of challenge.[17]

This setting can be excellent for gifted learners if the classroom teacher has training or expertise in differentiating instruction for the entire spectrum of learners and is knowledgeable about the characteristics and needs of gifted children.

Pull-out programs, where a gifted child is removed from his or her regular classroom for a period of time to receive instruction from a gifted education specialist, is perhaps the most popular service delivery model for high-ability learners. When working with the gifted education specialist, students often concentrate on work that is intended to enrich their education. Pull-out programs sometimes are designed to complement and supplement the work that occurs in the general education classroom, and sometimes not. Although the work addressed in pull-out settings often cuts across multiple disciplines, it is sometimes tailored to specific student needs, such as accelerated mathematics assignments for children who have demonstrated that they are able to handle additional challenge. The success of such services is, of course, highly dependent upon the abilities and skills of the teacher delivering the pull-out services.

Gifted education services also can be delivered through *special classes, special schools*, or other full-time or part-time settings targeted at gifted and highly talented students where they are grouped exclusively with their cognitive-ability peers or through acceleration, whereby gifted children advance one or multiple grade levels in a single subject or are promoted whole grades ahead so that they are placed with their cognitive group, rather than their age peers.[18] Such special classrooms and schools for the gifted have many benefits for students' cognitive development and academic performance, although some students resent or resist being separated from their age peers. Special classrooms may serve gifted children in a single grade, or may be configured to serve multiple ages. States and larger school districts also sometimes sponsor special schools that serve gifted and talented children. These special schools may focus on a specific area, such as the arts or science and technology, or they may concentrate instead on advanced learners. Special schools can be freestanding or housed in an existing school building where general education services are also offered. Special classrooms and schools often have the advantage of exposing children to teachers who have experience and expertise in working with gifted children as well as providing curricular materials that are often more advanced than those available in the general education classroom. While special classes and schools are highly effective, some children may find it difficult to adjust to separation from their age peers.

Some schools and school districts also offer early entrance to Kindergarten, single-subject acceleration, or grade skipping for gifted students. *Early entrance to Kindergarten* permits advanced learners to begin school at a younger age than is normally allowed, often after demonstrating advanced abilities through some type of assessment. *Single-subject acceleration* is designed to allow a child who is advanced in one area, such as mathematics, to join older children in an advanced grade for instruction in that subject rather than remaining with his or her classmates. *Grade skipping*, a more radical form of acceleration, has an advanced learner pass over one or more grades so that his or her learning needs will be better met. Acceleration is one of the most effective ways to support gifted learners, but remains unpopular with many teachers and administrators.

Special Needs

Some parents come to realize that their gifted child also has a learning disability or other special need, a condition known as being twice-exceptional. Twice-exceptional children can face difficulties in receiving the proper level of services, as their learning disability tends to mask their giftedness and vice versa. Some educators refer to twice-exceptional children as smart students who are not very good at school. How "not very good at school" is defined may vary. Some twice-exceptional students may receive passing and even above-average grades but not excel as one might expect, while others may fail some or most of their classes. Twice-exceptional children also must face the mindsets of some teachers who will not consider such learners for a gifted education program, because the teachers focus more on a child's skill deficiencies and overlook indicators of intellectual giftedness.

Twice-exceptional students frequently view themselves as deficient academically, which sometimes causes them to avoid schoolwork. Their experience with academics is often confusing, as many tasks are very easy for them to master, while others cause extreme difficulties. This confusion is often combined with unpleasant responses of teachers and parents, such as punishments for taking "too long" to complete work, failure in classes or grade retention, placement with developmentally delayed students, or negative reactions from teachers and peers. Modifications that are effective are assignments and projects that both recognize the twice-exceptional student's abilities yet also provide structure and strategies that will assist the student to accommodate weaknesses. It is also important to consider how identification processes in place will affect a child's diagnosis as being either gifted or possessing special needs.

If appropriate instruments are not used, twice-exceptional children will often receive inappropriate services. Parents will often need to work extensively with teachers and other school personnel to assure that their child's needs are met.

Other Approaches

Supplemental school and community programs. Services completely distinct and separate from school may also help gifted children develop their talents.[19] Saturday enrichment programs, summer camps, mentorships, clubs, and a host of other activities can supplement what a gifted child learns at school. Many school districts or colleges and universities offer such programming, but other organizations do as well. Public libraries, museums, symphony orchestras, park districts, opera companies, and other groups frequently offer programming for gifted children as a means of furthering their mission and performing public outreach. Indeed, because such out-of-school experiences can be tailored to a child's particular skills, interests, and talents they can be extremely valuable to his or her progress. Some programs designed to provide gifted children with these ancillary enrichment experiences are available at no cost or low cost. While children who live in urban or suburban areas have greater access to such programs, those who live in more isolated locations may be able to participate by means of online offerings.

Mentorships. Gifted children who have demonstrated a keen interest in a certain area of study or professional path, and who exhausted other opportunities provided by the school or other organizations offering programming for talented youth, could benefit from a mentoring relationship with a practitioner outside of the school. A mentorship is a vibrant shared relationship in which attitudes, passions, traditions, and values with regard to a field are passed from an older person to a younger colleague. These attitudes, passions, traditions, and values are shared and internalized, granting the mentee a better understanding of the field or profession, and helping him or her become a member of the group. Mentorships with artists, business people, scholars, or scientists are highly appropriate for gifted children with strong interest in a specific domain, particularly those who have mastered the essentials of the school curriculum or are interested in a field (e.g., aeronautics) not addressed in school. The process for acquiring a mentor for a gifted child has multiple components, and should be a joint effort between parents, teachers, and the child. This process entails:

- identifying the kinds of experiences that will benefit the child's talent development;
- deciding with the child whether he or she really wants a mentor;
- determining potential candidates to serve as a mentor;
- interviewing potential mentors to determine their interest in mentoring and fit for the child;
- establishing the expectations and parameters for the mentorship;
- preparing the gifted child for the mentorship; and
- monitoring the relationship to assure goals are being met.

Mentorships have been found to be especially useful for girls and gifted children from diverse backgrounds, as these relationships can help the child see possibilities for him- or herself that might otherwise not be realized. Mentorships are *not* appropriate or necessary for all gifted children, and should be judiciously used only in those cases where deep insights into a given field or domain would be helpful.

Homeschooling. Over the past 20 years, many parents have begun to homeschool their children.[20] The decision to homeschool one's child can stem from a variety of motivations, but dissatisfaction with available educational opportunities is a significant motivator. Parents of gifted children also decide to homeschool their children to find a better way to serve creative, intense, rapid, sensitive, and talented learners, to meet a child's unusual learning style, to offer programming unavailable in a classroom setting, or to sustain a love of learning.

- To make their homeschooling experience more successful, parents of gifted children should consider the following steps:

- Talk to other parents of gifted children who are homeschooling to discuss the challenges and rewards.

- Take the time to craft a mission statement that covers precisely what they want homeschooling to accomplish. This will help to clarify the reasons for homeschooling, the desired goals and outcomes, and the roles and responsibilities of various family members, and can be changed as a child's needs and interests evolve.

- Become familiar with their state's laws and regulations related to homeschooling to prevent problems later.

- Establish the relationships and schedule for homeschooling for each child. Homeschooling fosters a different relationship between parent and child than most are used to, and instituting roles and expectations for time spent working avoids problems later.

- Establish a customized curriculum plan for each child who will be homeschooled. While the plan is flexible and may change, it is beneficial to determine what will be covered during the academic year and to establish a rough calendar indicating how learning will proceed.

- Determine the gifted child's areas of strengths and weakness as well as passions and gaps in his or her learning. This will allow the child's education to be tailored to interests while also building competencies in areas that may not be as strong as desired.

Advocating for the Gifted Child

Choices related to the educational programming selected for gifted children are important, of great consequence, and momentous to a child's life. As a result, decisions related to programming options should be made only after careful consideration of available options. Sometimes parents will decide that they need to more strongly advocate for appropriate services for their child, gifted children, and particular programs. Advocacy occurs on various levels, including self, school, district, state, and national. While each of these levels has its own particular challenges and strategies, there are certain common themes that cross boundaries and allow change to proceed.

Most advocacy for gifted education begins when parents have concerns about their children's education and schooling.[21] This process begins with individual meetings with teachers or principals, then moves to larger conferences including administrators at school or district offices. Except for the earliest information-gathering meetings, the local advocacy process is much more effective when a gifted child's parents join with other parents to seek a desired result. Working with other parents allows the group to identify common concerns, develop common goals, and establish plans and strategies for action. Doing this as a group also permits the pooling of ideas and resources and the sharing of responsibilities.

When discussing matters related to gifted education with a superintendent or school board, it is important that the parent group establish the big picture at the outset, whether it be related to services offered, curriculum, identification procedures, or some other issue. The parent group needs to be able to go straight to the reason for their presentation and cite evidence that supports their request. Members of the parent group must be willing to take a strong stand on behalf of gifted children and request specific action. Given that school districts can be constrained by policies and procedures established by the state, some parents may decide that addressing these issues with members of the state legislature is an essential step. Local and statewide gifted organizations generally have legislative and advocacy committees and can provide parents with access to up-to-date information about their work and what efforts might already be under consideration by local/state legislative bodies. Through these efforts, many parent groups have affected the services provided not only their own children but all gifted learners.

Parent groups supporting gifted children already exist in many communities; some may be advisory groups to the local school district. For parents just becoming acquainted with gifted education, the National Association for Gifted Children or a state or local gifted education organization are the best places to begin. These groups have information on giftedness, laws and policies, downloadable materials, and other resources to help parents of gifted children become familiar with many of the issues facing gifted children and schools and they often have suggestions for effective advocacy. For those parents unable to find a group in their vicinity, starting a parent group that advocates for the needs of gifted children might be the right option. NAGC has a booklet on starting and sustaining a parent group that is freely available from the website.

Negotiating Programming Options

Bridget's parents should feel assured that they are already helping her to advance her many skills and talents. Since Bridget is 4, her parents should approach their local school district now to discuss what programming options are available to support their gifted daughter. If the district offers a school for advanced studies or other special classes, Bridget's parents should emphasize that her level of performance makes her a perfect candidate for such services. Bridget's parents should also inquire about having Bridget enter Kindergarten or first grade right now, based on her level of performance. They also should investigate Saturday programs that offer enrichment and participate as suitable in outreach programs available locally outside of school.

Alejandro's parents should ask his teacher about programming options that exist at his school. Certainly, Alejandro would benefit from pull-out programming and hopefully his classroom teacher is providing him with an appropriate level of challenge through differentiated instruction. Alejandro's parents may need to stress that while gifted, their son is also an English language learner (ELL), and will continue to be so. Many teachers do not have much training in working with ELLs and mistake the child's language status as evidence that he or she is not gifted. This is not the case, and Alejandro's parents need to be vigilant to ensure that his giftedness is recognized. Alejandro's proficiency in algebra makes him an excellent candidate for some form of acceleration. This programming option can take several forms, including grade-skipping, where Alejandro would be moved to a higher grade for all subjects, or single-subject acceleration, where he would focus on learning mathematics at a more advanced level while remaining with his age peers for other subjects. Many school districts do not promote acceleration options so Alejandro's parents might need to push for an evaluation of acceleration as an appropriate option with his teacher's assistance.

Like many schools located in rural areas, Christopher's school is unable to offer much in the way of formal programs for gifted children. After discussing programming options with Christopher's teacher and principal, his mother learns that his school district serves gifted children by having the classroom teachers differentiate instruction. The classroom teacher sometimes plans the instructional strategies she will use with Christopher and other gifted children with the district's gifted coordinator, who is housed in the central office and who serves all five elementary schools within the district. Christopher's mother knows that middle school teachers serve over 100 children per day, thus limiting the time they have to prepare instructional materials for the different needs of various groups. Through the school parent-teacher organization, his mother coordinates groups of parents to assist teachers in preparing materials to support differentiated instruction in the classrooms, helping to assure that quality differentiation takes place. Christopher's mother also meets with each of his teachers to ensure that she *understands how his work is being differentiated and how she can best support his learning at home.*

Kahlil's grandmother and mother should arrange a meeting with his school's principal to discuss appropriate placement options. If Kahlil's school district has a gifted education coordinator, she or he should also be included in the process. In particular, Kahlil's grandmother and mother should ask how he can be placed with other African American students or teachers so that he does not continue to feel isolated at school. Kahlil's grandmother and mother might suggest grade skipping that would permit him to work with older African American students on a regular basis. Kahlil's grandmother and mother might also have a conversation with him that emphasizes that sometimes we all need to make sacrifices in order to fully enjoy the long-term benefits of education. To the extent possible, Kahlil's grandmother and mother should also seek a mentor for Kahlil, perhaps from a local college or university or a Boys and Girls Club, who could allow him more opportunities to explore areas of interest or to exercise and build upon a skill or talent they have observed.

Je'Ana's parents have been mostly satisfied by the services their daughter has received. Although she has not always been fully challenged in school, her parents recognize that this is as much a consequence of Je'Ana's behavior as anything else. Because she has indicated a deep interest in writing, Je'Ana's parents might seek other options, such as dual enrollment, where a student takes a class at a college or university in lieu of a similar class offered at their high school. Je'Ana might enroll in a creative writing course at a nearby liberal arts college, where she will be able to earn college credit. As they begin her college search, Je'Ana's parents are also more interested in identifying schools that

41

are a good fit rather than those that are most highly ranked. Je'Ana is a student who thrives when she is motivated to embrace a subject, and she might do better at a college or university where she has a role in determining her course of study rather than one with a prescribed curriculum. Je'Ana also should explore colleges and universities that provide immersion terms in the arts, where students focus on theatrical productions or producing visual art for a semester at the exclusion of all other activity.

Suggestions

- Gifted children should not be asked to demonstrate mastery of fact-based information before entering gifted programs. Instead, the focus should be placed upon their ability to engage with and benefit from program offerings.

- Where differentiation in the general education classroom is the service model for gifted learners, parents should explore whether its effectiveness is being enhanced with flexible grouping, cluster grouping, continuity, and other instructional strategies that provide gifted children the opportunity to work with each other.

- Schools commonly use a variety of program models to organize their gifted education offerings, including the Autonomous Learner Model, the Schoolwide Enrichment Model, the Levels of Service approach, the Parallel Curriculum Model, and others with which parents may wish to become familiar so that they can offer support for their child and know what options are available;

- No program model can overcome an inappropriate curriculum or poor teaching. Quality implementation is a key to student success. Parents should support their teachers through the local parent/teacher organization and urge that all teachers receive regular professional development so that they are able to recognize and respond to the needs of gifted students.

- Parent groups can be a source of support, resources, and referrals in raising a gifted child. They also are instrumental in successful advocacy efforts to secure changes in the programs and services offered in the local schools. In addition to resources for parents at NAGC and other gifted education advocacy organizations, organizations such as the National Center for Learning Disabilities have specialized resources for parents of gifted children who also have a disability.[22]

- Homeschooling remains an option for parents who wish to pursue an alternate education approach that can address a child's skills and needs. Parents interested in homeschooling their gifted child might meet with some parents who are already homeschooling, both to learn about the option and to identify supports available in the area.

SOCIAL AND EMOTIONAL NEEDS

As do all children, gifted learners have social and emotional needs that must be met for them to fully enjoy their lives and reach their potential.[23] Certainly, gifted children may face a variety of potential social and emotional issues, but many parents are especially concerned with those involving perfectionism, the mixed messages that talented learners often receive, and issues relating to underachievement. Parents of a gifted child who is experiencing problems with any of these areas and who wish to guide and support their child's development should consult counselors, teachers, gifted education specialists, and others who might provide guidance and assistance related to their child's situation. Parents still must play a central role in dealing with social and emotional issues facing their children.

Perfectionism and Underachievement

Although several personality theorists believe it to be a healthy and salient part of human personality, perfectionism is most frequently thought of as a barrier to achievement and performance.[24] Perfectionism represents negative and destructive desires to have output meet an imagined ideal that results in the child being able to produce very little. As such, parents may see enabling perfectionism, which empowers the gifted learner to do his or her best work, or disabling perfectionism, which paralyzes performance and stymies productivity. Enabling perfectionism involves the sense of pleasure derived from the labors of painstaking effort and can be viewed as one of the motivators that encourage some to do an excellent job. Disabling perfectionism, conversely, causes the gifted child afflicted with it to be unable to derive satisfaction from his or her own work, because the work is never good enough to satisfy the child's own standards. A gifted child with disabling perfectionism often will be plagued with depression, guilt, and shame caused by his/her work and will often engage in procrastination, self-deprecation, and other face-saving behaviors to compensate. To avoid disabling perfectionism, parents of gifted children must be careful to avoid pressuring their gifted child to be perfect or to allow coaches or teachers to do so. Parents can also help their gifted children learn how to set appropriate goals and reflect on the value of mistakes.

Parents of gifted children sometimes struggle with those who are labeled underachievers, learners who exhibit an extreme discrepancy between their expected achievement (which is suggested by standardized achievement or IQ tests) and their actual achievement (performance as measured by grades and teacher assessments).[25] Sometimes underachievement can be the consequence of some emotional, mental, or physical problem—parents should always check with their child's pediatrician to rule this out when faced with underachievement before taking other steps. Many times, however, underachievement is caused by the gifted child's attitudes, motivation, and perceptions. Attitudes toward school, teachers, and classes involve interest in and affect toward these factors. Those gifted students who are disinterested in the subject studied, who have problems with authority figures, or who express other negative attitudes are more likely to be underachievers than their peers who have more positive attitudes.

Parents and families that seek to address underachievement in a gifted child might consider interventions to address this situation. Interventions

45

directed at underachievement fall under either counseling or changes in instructional practices. Counseling interventions work to change personal or family dynamics and to address the ambitions of both. Counseling may focus on the child, his or her family, or all involved in a group session. The counselor's goal is not to compel the underachiever to become a more successful student, but instead to help him or her determine whether success is a desirable goal. If the child decides success is a desirable goal, the counselor then assists in reversing counterproductive attitudes and work habits. Instructional interventions often involve the establishment of special classrooms for gifted underachievers with lower teacher to student ratio. In this setting, the teacher can create less conventional teaching and learning activities, offer students more choice and control of their learning, and modify assessments and learning strategies to better meet the gifted underachievers' needs. All school-centered interventions need to include input and buy-in from students, parents, and school personnel so that efforts may be unified and seamless.

Family structure, climate, and values all can affect a gifted child's achievement.[26] Extreme amounts of early attention, for example, may create attention dependence, where children become frozen when asked to perform independently. Similarly, the parents who fail to create a positive home atmosphere are more likely to have their gifted children underachieve, as are those who show little interest in education. Consistency between the gifted child's parents is more critical to that child's achievement than any particular style of parenting, and families that are well-organized seem to better foster achievement in their children.

Other Concerns

Gifted learners often receive mixed messages regarding their skills and talents. Most desire normal social interactions with their age peers, yet also believe others will treat them differently if they display their giftedness. As a result of these perspectives, gifted children frequently learn how to play different social roles with different audiences in different social settings. To better support their gifted children, parents must learn about their social goals and examine how these fit with their personalities. Parents can also provide opportunities for their children to better understand themselves and arrange meetings with other gifted children. Other parenting strategies for gifted children are not so different than those any parent uses—adults should model the behaviors they want their children to exhibit and not try to change their basic nature. Gifted children's parents should encourage their sons and daughters to enjoy nonacademic interests and to appreciate down time. With these supports in place, many gifted children will thrive and excel.

Gifted Children's Social and Emotional Lives

Bridget's parents allow her time to pursue her interests in Bach and the solar system, subscribing to a chamber orchestra concert series and accompanying their daughter to a nearby planetarium. Because they also realize that she is 4, however, they appreciate her thrilled reaction to the sandbox they installed behind their house and seek to expose her to great children's literature that is age appropriate in theme. Bridget's mother and father enjoy allowing her to help with chores around the house and give her small tasks, such as setting the table, which she enjoys immensely. Although Bridget's parents take time to arrange play dates for her with

47

other neighborhood children who are her age, they also enroll her in a creative writing program for gifted children where she is the youngest child enrolled by several years. In all other things, Bridget's parents seek to achieve a balance between her cognitive abilities and chronological age.

Alejandro's mother and father are proud of his excellent grades and his many interests. Despite this, they appreciate that he is an 8-year-old boy and encourage him to participate in and enjoy activities with other third graders. To this end, Alejandro's father helps to coach his soccer team and his mother makes sure that he plays frequently with his cousins who are the same age. Although Alejandro speaks English better than either of his parents, they also try to minimize the times where he is needed to act as an interpreter or translator, using neighbors and friends where possible. Alejandro's parents take the time to enroll him in a Junior Great Books program conducted at a local college and allow him to join a summer math camp held at the middle school. In this way, Alejandro is able to develop his cognitive skills while also enjoying life as a little boy.

Christopher has demonstrated well-above average performance in the classroom and extraordinary accomplishments on the playing fields and with musical instruments. Observing that Christopher thrives in an environment where he works with other children, his mother might consider getting him involved in a band, orchestra, or other musical group so that he may develop these skills while engaging with other children. It is important for all working with Christopher to remember that he exhibits asynchronous development, insofar that his cognitive performance is that of a 15 year old, his physical accomplishments are similar to those of a 16 year old, but his social and emotional maturity is that of an 11 year old. A mixed-age ensemble might work best for Christopher, as it would permit his cognitive and affective needs to be met, albeit through different children. Christopher would be well-served if his mother permits him to determine the genre of music to be played, so that bluegrass, classical, or jazz groups might all be appropriate. Allowing Christopher this choice will increase his ownership of his participation and increase the likelihood that his involvement will be successful.

Kahlil's grandmother and mother have discussed with him his desire to spend more time with neighborhood children and their concomitant intention that he seek to develop his many gifts. While Kahlil's grandmother and mother balked at permitting him to join the middle school football team because they feared possible injury, they compromised and agreed that he could play basketball and run track with his school teams. Kahlil has also enjoyed immensely the transfer to a racially mixed magnet school where he does not feel so isolated from other children like him. Because his teachers allow him to pursue guided investigations into matters that are of great interest to him, such as jazz, physics, and slam poetry, Kahlil has become engrossed in his studies and is more interested in his academic work and happier with his social life than ever before.

Although she performs well in school now, when Je'Ana was younger she was an underachiever academically. Happily, Je'Ana's middle school mathematics teacher, Mr. White, noticed that her achievement test scores indicated she performed at the 99th percentile in that subject, even though her grades were mediocre at best. Underachievement has many causes, but sometimes it is created by boredom that stems from coursework that is too easy for the gifted learner. After Mr. White changed the work that Je'Ana was doing to problem-based exercises that used mathematical concepts from three grades above her placement, her performance improved dramatically. Math did not become Je'Ana's favorite subject, but her grades increased from the low-80s to the high-90s on tests and she came to enjoy some aspects of playing with numbers.

Suggestions

- Remember that advanced cognitive development does not equate with high levels of social or emotional development. A brilliant child may act in age appropriate ways or be quite immature;

- When gifted children are grouped with their age peers, they may find few friends who are similar in cognitive ability, and thus they may relate to them better in non-academic ways. Gifted children may need to join clubs or organizations or attend weekend and summer programs where they can interact with older children to find others who share their abilities and academic interests.

- Society's failure to value differences, including positive difference, will often cause gifted individuals adjustment problems. Discussing this incongruity will assist the gifted child in dealing with it;

- Disabling perfectionism is a characteristic of some gifted children and can be a serious and constraining problem that inhibits trying new experiences because of a fear of failure. Setting reasonable expectations and praising effort rather than results will counter this.

- Gifted children may experience different social and emotional consequences than their age peers, a situation that is neither good nor bad but one that must be considered when adjustment issues arise. Teachers, counselors, and others will sometimes need to be reminded of this.

- Gifted children who have strong self-esteem often acquire a sense of independence, demonstrate exploratory behavior, become self-assertive, exhibit a strong inner locus of control, and show greater self-trust. Parents should support their gifted child's self-esteem by allowing him or her to work to develop skills and competencies of which the child and family can be proud.

CONCLUSION

Parenting gifted children, much like experiences rearing all children, requires a consistent balance between cognitive, social and emotional, and physical needs. Gifted children's parents need to understand and push for programs and services through their local schools. Using afterschool, Saturday, summer, and other programs for gifted learners can help parents find the right mix for their children. Parents who understand and respond to the characteristics and differing developmental patterns of gifted learners, the various programming options available to support their growth, and the special social and emotional characteristics of their own children will greatly increase their children's rates of adjustment and academic success. Often, this journey will be easier if parents join together with the parents of other gifted children both to exchange ideas and to act as a resource when certain issues arise. Together, parents of gifted children also will find that it is easier to affect change and influence decision makers, as there is power in numbers.

Parenting gifted children can be especially time consuming, and it is sometimes difficult to find resources that are appropriate for them The rewards for doing so, however, are immense and there are many resources that can assist parents in their efforts. Parents who work with teachers and others to support their gifted children will find that such efforts can make a tremendous positive difference.

Parenting Gifted Children

Bridget is thriving as she prepares to enter school. Delighted to pursue her interests in the solar system and music, she has begun violin lessons taught by a local teacher and enjoys a Saturday enrichment program where she attends science-related classes. Although her educational attainments are many, Bridget also enjoys playing with other 4-year-olds and views her older sisters as mentors and models for things she wants to do. Bridget's parents have become members of both a local gifted association and NAGC and have enjoyed networking with other parents who share similar challenges and concerns. As Bridget grows older, her parents are committed to providing her continued challenges and enrichment.

Alejandro has always done well in school, but his parents worried if they were adequately supporting his learning needs. After joining a bilingual gifted parents group, Alejandro's parents are much more confident they are doing all they can for their son. Alejandro has begun going to local museums with his mother, who initially was worried that her lack of English would impede his learning. The visits have shown her that being able to discuss the exhibits with Alejandro has greatly increased his understanding of what he sees. As she asks Alejandro to describe what he has seen and to compare and contrast various exhibits, Alejandro's mother is assisting him to better interact with the world around him. Alejandro's father has also begun volunteering in his classroom, which provides him with a better understanding of what Alejandro is studying and demonstrates his high regard for education to his son.

Christopher has excelled in athletics and academics. Despite this, his mother has been concerned that her financial situation and time constraints will negatively impact Christopher's future performance. By examining her situation, she has come to see that her work schedule, although difficult, provides her increased opportunities to interact with her children and to provide them with academic and social and emotional support and guidance. In an effort to expand Christopher's educational options, his mother is working with other parents and his teachers to ensure that differentiated instruction occurs in his classrooms. Additionally, in order to acknowledge Christopher's musical talents, as well as his asynchronous development, his mother is working to find a mixed-age musical group so that he can pursue his interest in music in an environment that supports his social and emotional needs.

Kahlil has on occasion struggled with his sense of identity and has not always been sure of who he wants to be. While he enjoys learning and the stimulation provided him in his honors classes, he also longs to be accepted as a member of his peer group. Kahlil's grandmother and mother have worked to find him mentors at his church and in his community who buttress his confidence and motivate him to do well academically. By helping Kahlil transfer to a magnet school with many gifted children of color, his grandmother and mother have helped him establish a group of academically minded friends. His grandmother's and mother's willingness to adjust Kahlil's experiences to better meet his interests and learning style have helped him adjust while their nonnegotiable stance on the importance of his education has helped him to appreciate and understand the opportunities he has to build a great future.

Je'Ana performs best when she is motivated, which occurs most frequently when she is interested in the subject and challenged at an appropriate level. Je'Ana's parents have nurtured her interest in English, social studies, and the arts by encouraging her work on the school newspaper, in theatre productions, and attend a summer camp for budding journalists. Je'Ana's parents also have joined a group of parents of the gifted, which has given them suggestions regarding how best to motivate their child. As Je'Ana begins her college search, she is sure in her passions and is willing to take appropriate risks to get where she wants to go after graduation. As someone who is passionately interested in language and the arts, Je'Ana decides to focus her college search primarily on institutions that are especially strong in these areas as she intends to major in English, art, media studies, or a similar field.

Suggestions

- On occasion gifted children may experience different social and emotional issues and challenges than do their non-gifted age peers;

- Gifted children sometimes demonstrate affective or physical maturity that is asynchronous with their cognitive abilities, indicating that parents should always consider the child's chronological age when making decisions;

- Intrinsic motivation can be fostered by permitting for flexible deadlines, eliminating overt supervision, and encouraging choices to be made by the gifted child;

- Unhealthy perfectionism can be a serious and limiting problem for a gifted child, insofar that it discourages them from trying new activities and experiences due to a fear of failure; and

- Underachievement is often a side effect of unhealthy perfectionism and can often escape detection by school authorities as a child's giftedness permits him or her to perform at or above grade level, even while not living up to his or her potential.

ENDNOTES

[1] We are sensitive to the certainty that many gifted children are raised in homes where the grandparents, other relatives, foster care guardians, or other guardians may have primary or sole responsibility for decision-making for the gifted child. However, for ease of reading we have elected to use the terms parent and parenting throughout this publication. We hope you will recognize that no disrespect for all of those other caregivers is intended.

[2] There are a variety of conceptions of giftedness. Those interested in exploring some of the more influential viewpoints might read, Borland, J. H. (2005). Gifted education without gifted children: The case for no conception of giftedness. In R. J. Sternberg & J. E. Davidson (Eds.), *Conceptions of giftedness* (2nd ed., pp. 1-19). New York, NY: Cambridge University Press; Davis, Callahan, C. M., & Miller, E. M. (2005). A child-responsive model of giftedness. In R. J. Sternberg (Ed.), *Conceptions of giftedness* (2nd ed., pp. 38-51). New York, NY: Cambridge University Press; G. A. (2006). *Gifted children and gifted education: A handbook for teachers and parents*. Scottsdale, AZ: Great Potential Press; Renzulli, J. S. (1988). A decade of dialogue on the three-ring conception of giftedness. *Roeper Review, 11*(1), 18-25; Stanley, J. C. (1980). On educating the gifted. *Educational Researcher, 9*(3), 8-12; and Sternberg, R. J. (1996). Myths, countermyths, and truths about intelligence. *Educational Researcher, 25*(2), 11-16.

[3] Complete citations to the research upon which many points are based are beyond the scope of the works in the NAGC Select series. For those readers interested in the research studies that have provided the field of gifted education with much of what is known about how to best support gifted children, we suggest Plucker and Callahan's *Critical Issues and Practices in Gifted Education: What the Research Says* (2nd ed.), which is listed in the resources section of this work. This being the case, we will provide a handful of citations by means of endnotes that provide readers useful starting points to learn more about the research undergirding the knowledge base of gifted education. The characteristics and needs of gifted learners, and how these differ from those of their age peers, have been well documented. See, e.g., Clark, B. (2014). *Growing up gifted* (8th ed.). Upper Saddle River, NJ: Pearson; and Passow, A. H., & Frasier, M. M. (1996). Toward improving identification of talent potential among minority and disadvantaged students. *Roeper Review, 18*(3), 198-202.

[4] Those interested in reviewing some of these different conceptions of giftedness might read Sternberg, R. J., & Davidson, J. E. (Eds.). (2005). *Conceptions of giftedness* (2nd ed.). New York, NY: Cambridge University Press.

[5] Those wanting to increase their understanding of creative thinking and problem solving skills might review Csikszentmihalyi, M. (1996). *Creativity: Flow and the psychology of discovery and invention*. New York, NY: HarperCollins Publishers; or Treffinger, D. J., Isaksesen, S. G., & Stead-Dorval, K. B. (2006). *Creative problem solving: An introduction* (4th ed.). Waco, TX: Prufrock Press.

[6] Some superb sources that explore these differences include, Ford, D. Y., & Harris, J. J. (1999). *Multicultural gifted education*. New York, NY: Teachers College Press; Frasier, M. M., & Passow, A. H. (1994). *Toward a new paradigm for identifying talent potential* (Research Monograph 94112). Storrs: University of Connecticut, National Research Center on the Gifted and Talented; Perry, T., Steele, C., & Hilliard III, A. (2003). *Young, gifted, and black: Promoting high*

achievement among African American students. Boston, MA: Beacon Press; and Reis, S. M., & Small, M. A. (2005). The varied and unique characteristics exhibited by diverse gifted and talented learners. In F. A. Karnes, & S. M. Bean (Eds.), *Methods and materials for teaching the gifted* (2nd ed., pp. 3-35). Waco, TX: Prufrock Press.

[7] See Ford, D. Y. (2013). *Recruiting & retaining culturally different students in gifted education*. Waco, TX: Prufrock Press.

[8] Appropriate activities for young gifted learners are discussed in Smutny, J. F., & von Fremd, S. (Eds.). (2010). *Differentiating for the young gifted child: Teaching strategies across the content areas, PreK-3* (2nd ed.). Thousand Oaks, CA: Corwin Press.

[9] Bloom, B. S. (1964). *Subtlety and change in human characteristics*. New York, NY: Wiley; and Montessori, M. (1966). *The secret of childhood*. Notre Dame, IN: Fides Publishers.

[10] Discussions related to academic fit, and issues that can arise can be found in Colangelo, N., Assouline, S. G., & Gross, M. U. M. (2004). *A nation deceived: How schools hold back America's brightest students*. Iowa City: University of Iowa, Belin - Blank International Center for Gifted Education and Talent Development; Renzulli, J. S., & Reis, S. M. (2014). *The schoolwide enrichment model: A how-to guide for talent development* (3rd ed.). Waco, TX: Prufrock Press; Smutny, J. F., Walker, S. Y., & Honeck, I. E. (2015). *Teaching gifted children in today's preschool and primary classrooms: Identifying, nurturing, and challenging children ages 4–9*. Minneapolis, MN: Free Spirit; Stanley, J. C., & Benbow, C. P. (1982). Educating mathematically precocious youths: Twelve policy recommendations. *Educational Researcher, 11*(5), 4-9; and Treffinger, D. J., Young, G. C., Nassab, C. A., & Wittig, C. V. (2004). *Expanding and enhancing gifted education programs: The levels of service approach*. Waco, TX: Prufrock Press.

[11] Additional information about home dynamics may be found at Freeman, J. (2013). The long-term effects of families and educational provision on gifted children. *Educational & Child Psychology, 30*(2), 7-17; McGee, C. D., & Hughes, C. E. (2011). Identifying and supporting young gifted learners. *YC: Young Children, 66*(4), 100-105; Olszewski-Kubilius, P. (2014). Family environment and social development in gifted students. *Gifted Child Quarterly, 58*, 199-216; Rimm, S., & Lowe, B. (1988). Family environments of underachieving gifted children. *Gifted Child Quarterly, 32*, 353-359. Those interested in a more detailed exploration of the studies that identified parenting styles might review Steinberg, L., Lamborn, S. D., Dornbusch, S. M., & Darling, N. (1992). Impact of parenting practices on adolescent achievement: Authoritative parenting, school involvement, and encouragement to succeed, *Child Development, 63*(5), 1266-1281.

[12] Additional reading about what is known, and what is not known, regarding family composition may be found in Plucker, J. A., & Callahan, C. M. (2014). Research on giftedness and gifted education: Status of the field and considerations for the future. *Exceptional Children, 80*(4), 390-406; Robinson, N. M. (1993). *Parenting the very young, gifted child* (RBDM 9308). Storrs: University of Connecticut, National Research Center on the Gifted and Talented.

[13] More about parent experiences with groups may be found in Matthews, M. S., Georgiades, S. D., & Smith, L. F. (2011). How we formed a parent advocacy group and what we've learned in the process. *Gifted Child Today, 34*(4), 28-34; and Weber, C. L., & Stanley, L. (2012). Educating parents of gifted children: Designing effective workshops for changing parent perceptions.

Gifted Child Today, 35(2), 128-136. See also a free, downloadable publication, *Starting & Sustaining a Parent Group to Support Gifted Children*, available from NAGC at www.nagc.org.

[14] Additional background reading regarding parenting support may be found in Jolly, J. L., & Matthews, M. S. (2012). A critique of the literature on parenting gifted learners. *Journal for the Education of the Gifted, 35*(3), 260-290; and Jolly, J. L., Treffinger, D. J., Inman, T. F., & Smutny, J. F. (Eds.). (2011). Parenting gifted children. Waco, TX: Prufrock Press.

[15] More about achieving this balance can be found in Gallagher, J. J. (2015). Psychology, psychologists, and gifted students. *Journal for the Education of the Gifted, 38*(1), 6-17; and Garn, A. C., Matthews, M. S., & Jolly, J. L. (2012). Parents' role in the academic motivation of students with gifts and talents. *Psychology in the Schools, 49*(7), 656-667.

[16] Further information on programming options can be found at Schroth, S. T. (2014). Service delivery models, in J. A. Plucker & C. M. Callahan (Eds.), *Critical issues and practices in gifted education: What the research says* (2nd ed., pp. 577-592), Waco, TX: Prufrock Press; and Young, M. H., & Balli, S. J. (2014) Gifted and talented education (GATE): Student and parent perspectives. *Gifted Child Today, 37*(4), 236-246.

[17] Further reading on differentiated instruction, and ways to implement it with gifted learners include Tomlinson, C. A. (2003). *Fulfilling the promise of the differentiated classroom: Strategies and tools for responsive teaching*. Alexandria, VA: Association for Supervision and Curriculum Development; and Tomlinson, C. A., Kaplan, S. N., Renzulli, J. S., Purcell, J. H., Leppien, J. H., Burns, D. E., Strickland, C. A., & Imbeau, M. B. (2008). *The parallel curriculum: A design to develop learner potential and challenge advanced learners*. Thousand Oaks, CA: Corwin Press.

[18] Some of the more well-known program models for gifted education include Betts, G. T., & Kercher, J. K. (1999). *Autonomous learner model: Optimizing ability*. Greeley, CO: ALPS; Renzulli, J. S., & Reis, S. M. (2014). *The schoolwide enrichment model: A how-to guide for talent development* (3rd ed.). Waco, TX: Prufrock Press; Treffinger, D. J., Young, G. C., Nassab, C. A., & Wittig, C. V. (2004). *Enhancing and expanding gifted programs: The levels of service approach*. Waco, TX: Prufrock Press. Special schools for gifted children are looked at broadly in Coleman, L. J., & Cross, T. L. (2005). *Being gifted in school: An introduction to development, guidance, and teaching*. Waco, TX: Prufrock Press and in depth in Coleman, L. J. (2005). *Nurturing talent in high school: Life in the fast lane*. New York, NY: Teachers College Press. Those interested in a detailed argument for the acceleration of bright children might also review Assouline, S. G., Colangelo, N., VanTassel-Baska, J., & Lupkowski-Shoplik, A. (2015). *A nation empowered: Evidence trumps the excuses for holding back America's brightest students*. Iowa City: University of Iowa, Belin - Blank International Center for Gifted Education and Talent Development. .

[19] Those interested in information about Saturday and summer enrichment programs and other activities that occur outside of school might review Schroth, S. T., (2007). Selecting afterschool programs: A guide for parents. *Parenting for High Potential*, 21-30; and Kaul, C. R., Johnson, S. K., Witte, M. M., & Saxon, T. F. (2015). Critical components of summer enrichment program for urban low-income gifted students. *Gifted Child Today, 38*(1), 32-40. A detailed discussion of when mentoring might be appropriate may be found at Callahan, C. M., & Dickson, R. K. (2014) Mentors & mentorships. In J.

A. Plucker & C. M. Callahan (Eds.), *Critical issues and practices in gifted education* (2nd ed., pp. 413-426). Waco, TX: Prufrock Press.

[20] More information about homeschooling may be found at, Jolly, J. L., Matthews, M. S., & Nester, J. (2013). Homeschooling the gifted: A parent's perspective. Gifted Child Quarterly, 57, 121-134.

[21] Readings regarding advocacy for gifted children include, Duquette, C., Orders, S., Fullerton, S., & Robertson-Grewal, K. (2011). Fighting for their rights: Advocacy experiences of parents of children identified with intellectual giftedness. *Journal for the Education of the Gifted, 34*(3), 488-512 and Wiskow, K., Fowler, V. D., & Christopher, M. M. (2011). Working together for appropriate services for gifted learners. *Gifted Child Today, 34*(2), 20-25. See also NAGC's online advocacy resources at www.nagc.org.

[22] Information regarding the National Center for Learning Disabilities may be found at http://www.ncld.com; materials related to twice-exceptional learners can also be found at the National Research Center on the Gifted and Talented at http://www.gifted.uconn.edu/nrcgt/.

[23] A variety of superb resources exist for those wanting to learn more about these issues, including Cross, T. L. (2011). *Social and emotional lives of gifted children* (4th ed.). Waco, TX: Prufrock Press and Niehart, M., Pfeiffer, S., & Cross, T. L. (Eds.). (2016). *The social and emotional development of gifted children: What do we know?* (2nd ed.). Waco, TX: Prufrock Press.

[24] More information about perfectionism can be obtained by reading Dabrowski, K. (1972). *Psychoneurosis is not an illness*. London, England: Little, Brown; Greenspon, T. S., (2012). Perfectionism: A counselor's role in a recovery process, in T. L. Cross & J. R. Cross (Eds.), *Handbook for counselors serving students with gifts and talents: Development, relationships, school issues and counseling needs/interventions* (pp. 597-614). Waco, TX: Prufrock Press; Nugent, S. (2000). Perfectionism: Its manifestations and classroom-based interventions. *Journal of Secondary Gifted Education, 12*, 215-221.

[25] More information about underachievement may be found at Reis, S. M., & McCoach, D. B. (2002). Underachievement in gifted students, in M. Neihart, S. M. Reis, N. M. Robinson, & S. M. Moon (Eds.), *The social and emotional development of gifted children: What do we know?* (pp. 81-91). Waco, TX: Prufrock Press; and Yssel, N. (2012). Twice-exceptional students, in T. L. Cross & J. R. Cross (Eds.), *Handbook for counselors serving students with gifts and talents: Development, relationships, school issues and counseling needs/interventions* (pp. 245-260). Waco, TX: Prufrock Press.

[26] Further reading should include Hermann, K. M., & Lawrence, C. (2012). Family relationships, in T. L. Cross & J. R. Cross (Eds.), *Handbook for counselors serving students with gifts and talents: Development, relationships, school issues and counseling needs/interventions* (pp. 393-408). Waco, TX: Prufrock Press.

RESOURCES

Parents of gifted children, teachers of the gifted, administrators, and other interested parties often have questions regarding how best to parent a gifted child. The following resources provide a place to begin to find answers to many common questions.

Print Resources

Adams, C. M., & Chandler, K. L. (Eds.). (2014). *Effective program models for gifted students from underserved populations*. Waco, TX: Prufrock Press. Clear and concise review of best practices for serving underserved populations of gifted learners, such as children of color, English language learners, and students from low-SES backgrounds.

Callahan, C. M., & Hertberg-Davis, H. L. (Eds.). (2013). *Fundamentals of gifted education: Considering multiple perspectives*. New York, NY: Routledge. Strong resource covering all aspects of gifted education from a scholarly perspective.

Clark, B. (2014). *Growing up gifted: Developing the potential of children at school and at home* (8th ed.). Upper Saddle River, NJ: Pearson. A classic and highly accessible overview of parenting and teaching gifted children, written in a clear, concise, and convincing manner.

Jolly, J., Treffinger, D. J., Inman, T. F., & Smutny, J. F. (Eds.). (2011). *Parenting gifted children*. Waco, TX: Prufrock Press. Collection of some of the best articles from *Parenting for High Potential*, a leading magazine for parents of gifted children published by NAGC.

Neihart, M., Pfeiffer, S., & Cross, T. L. (Eds.). (2016). *The social and emotional development of gifted children: What do we know?*(2nd ed.). Waco, TX: Prufrock Press. Practical and useful overview of many issues related to the social and emotional needs of gifted children.

Plucker, J. A., & Callahan, C. M. (Eds.). (2014). *Critical issues and practices in gifted education: What the research says* (2nd ed). Waco, TX: Prufrock Press. Summary of the research undergirding gifted education, providing an objective analysis and evaluation of the available knowledge on a variety of topics related to instructional strategies, giftedness, and talent development.

Robinson, A., Shore, B. M., & Enersen, D. L. (2007). *Best practices in gifted education: An evidence-based guide*. Waco, TX: Prufrock Press. Research-based primer on best practices for gifted education programs.

Smutny, J. F., & von Fremd, S. E. (2010). *Differentiating for the young child: Teaching strategies across the content areas, K–3* (2nd ed.). Thousand Oaks, CA: Corwin Press. Wonderful suggestions for working with younger gifted learners, with many ideas for supporting these children in the classroom and home.

Tomlinson, C. A. (1999). *The differentiated classroom: Responding to the needs of all learners*. Alexandria, VA: Association for Supervision and Curriculum Development. Classic explanation of the principles undergirding differentiated instruction and practical ways of using this with children.

Treffinger, D. J., Schoonover, P. F., & Selby, E. C. (2013). *Educating for creativity and innovation: A comprehensive guide for research-based practice*. Waco, TX: Prufrock Press. Excellent overview of the scholarship related to building critical and creative thinking skills and practical suggestions to do so.

VanTassel-Baska, J. L., Cross, T. L., & Olenchak, F. R. (Eds.). (2009). *Social-emotional curriculum with gifted and talented students*. Waco, TX: Prufrock Press. A comprehensive guide to enhancing gifted children's social and emotional development for parents, counselors, teachers, and others interested in their well-being.

Electronic Resources

Association for Library Service to Children—a division of the American Library Association (ALA) lists award-winning children's literature and other resources http://www.ala.org/alsc/

History for Kids—a group of websites identified by the ALA as having excellent resources http://gws.ala.org/category/history-biography

Kids.gov—official United States government website with a variety of activities, games, and lesson plans related to art, history, reading, science, and other subjects http://kids.usa.gov/parents/index.shtml

Kids Public Radio—three advertising-free audio networks with stories, music (in English and Spanish), and lullabies ideal for younger listeners http://www.kidspublicradio.org/

Lyric Opera of Chicago—makes available a variety of lesson plans, materials, and tools helpful for exposing children to music http://www.lyricopera.org/

Metropolitan Museum of Art—resources available include timeline, downloadable images of collections, and other materials http://www.metmuseum.org/

National Association for Gifted Children (NAGC)— provides a variety of resources for parents and teachers, including research, networks, and materials, as well as links to state organizations http://www.nagc.org/

Science for Kids—includes games, experiments, and videos related to science for a variety of age groups http://www.sciencekids.co.nz/

Smithsonian Institution—provides access to activities and collections as well as links to the many Smithsonian museums, including the African American History & Culture Museum, the Air and Space Museum, the American Indian Museum, the Freer Gallery of Art, the Natural History Museum, the National Zoo, and the National History Museum http://www.si.edu/

Supporting Emotional Needs of the Gifted (SENG)—an organization devoted to gifted children's social and emotional has a website with links to research, support groups, and other materials of interest to parents http://www.sengifted.org/

ABOUT THE AUTHORS

Stephen T. Schroth holds a Ph.D. in educational psychology/gifted education from the University of Virginia. Dr. Schroth is an associate professor of early childhood education at Towson University. The author and editor of multiple books, monographs, book chapters, articles, and other publications, he has been a classroom teacher, gifted coordinator, and arts prototype school coordinator for a decade in the Los Angeles Unified School District. His research interests include early childhood education, the development of artistically talented students, differentiated instruction, learning styles, teacher education, creativity and problem solving, effective instructional and leadership practices, and working with English language learners. He is a past-chair of the NAGC Arts Network.

Jason A. Helfer holds a Ph.D. in curriculum and instruction from the University of Illinois. Dr. Helfer serves as Assitant Superintendent of Teacher & Leader Effectiveness for the Illinois State Board of Education. After serving as a classroom teacher for the Evanston/Skokie Community Consolidated School District 65 in Illinois and for the Grapevine/Colleyville Independent School District in Texas, he worked for more than a decade in higher education. The author of a series of curricular materials for the Lyric Opera of Chicago (with S. Schroth), Dr. Helfer is interested in rigorous curriculum, teacher education, and diverse learners.

ABOUT THE SERIES EDITOR

Cheryll M. Adams, Ph.D., is the director emerita of the Center for Gifted Studies and Talent Development at Ball State University. She has served on the Board of Directors of NAGC and has been president of the Indiana Association for the Gifted and the Association for the Gifted, Council for Exceptional Children.